Stars like the Sun

Rithika Thomas

BookLeaf Publishing

Presentation by *BookLeaf Publishing*

Web: www.bookleafpub.com

E-mail: info@bookleafpub.com

ISBN: 9789357213301

First edition 2023

dreams

her dreams lay beyond an unseen horizon,
the edge of the world a harsh line,
a reminder of where reality lies waiting.

her dreams lay beyond an unseen horizon,
like the shadow of herself beneath the sun,
a sure existence, visible yet intangible.

her dreams lay beyond an unseen horizon,
across a sea of possibilities,
the waves of challenges a brute force.

so she built herself a boat and sailed
and with every wave she conquered,
the horizon seemed tangible.
- a fighter till the end.

dandelion soul

delicate as she seems
there is a spirit stronger than most
within her that lives
and leaves its trails
like a dandelion.

but she is indeed fragile,
you can shake her all you like
even the mightiest quake
could not break her,
like a dandelion.

I can let you in on a secret:
all it takes is a sharp,
deliberate breath in the wrong direction
and you will see the life
fade away into the breeze.
- she is strong, but fragile.

asteroids

to create is to plunge
into that deep, dark void
of pain and sorrow and heartbreaks.

you find pieces of yourself
much like those of a broken planet
roaming the solar system.

they are your mosaic tiles
that are forged together
to create unforgettable art.

and sometimes, it leaves you
drained and unfulfilled,
without aim; an asteroid in the void.

it is draining to bring out
emotions you would rather
forget than ever relive.

but you have seen asteroids,
once their aim is true
they burn and burn and burn
- until it is all gone.

the pit

it sits tightly wound
everywhere and nowhere
all at once,
it comes and goes
in hot and cold flashes
the hair on my arms standing.

it uncoils and coils
a snake threatened in its nest
hissing to defend itself,
my body is trembling
but the source of the fear
is unknown.

a whirlpool of thoughts
in my head
a sure weight squatted
on my chest.

as my heart thunders
like a thousand wings
held captive in a cage
and my body trembles
like a tree defenceless
in the eye of a storm

i obsessively wonder
when will this storm calm down?
because I've had enough
of this uncertainty.
- sometimes it is a calamity.

stress does not make

every functioning thing requires fuel
and movement that squeaks with rust
must be oiled regularly
because what else are you
if not a machine made to work
ridiculously hard under pressure.
- machines and humans are the same.

her

her legs trembled beneath her
like they would soon give out
and she would crumble to the ground.

it took every ounce of her will
to remain resilient and steadfast
a fire in her chest unsurpassed.

she was tested, over and over,
obstacles strewed in her sight
like dead petals on a winter night

but not once did she look back,
as she braved the tempest
with a promise at the end to rest.
- there is a calm before the storm, what about
after?

falling apart together

sometimes you need to fall apart
because certain pieces have yet
to find their right places within you.

there are jigsaws that are incomplete
with pieces that are missing,
and pieces that do not fit.

you need to fall apart
so the jigsaw pieces of your heart
can fall together in a perfect mosaic.

you can paint a beautiful portrait
but they are always incomplete
without the eyes, or nose, or lips.

sometimes you need to fall apart
more than once to create
that beautiful jigsaw and portrait.

your heart cannot be right every time;
a jigsaw piece might not fit
or it might be a wrong stroke of the brush.

but just the way others make mistakes,
your heart makes them too.
- there is refuge in lessons.

self-hate/love

it used to scare me to think
of going through days by myself
when every reflection
was an ashen face
with sunken, vacant eyes.

my lips would tremble
swollen and red and dry
echoing the state of my eyes
every other night
when I fought her in the mirror.

it used to scare me to think
I would have to face her
one day and perhaps
spend days and nights
nursing her to health.

but I realised
that girl in the mirror
was as harmless as I was.
who seemed to ask for nothing
beyond some help and love.
- from the girl beyond the mirror.

declaration

it is a declaration beyond measure
to gather the stars, the sky
the moon and the sun
only to give it to that one
who holds your heart in their hands.
it is a declaration of everything
you are willing to give
while expecting nothing in return.
- a dangerous declaration.

broken record

there is only back and forth
from the bed to the table
the room to the kitchen
the dorm to my childhood room
one country to another.

neither is home, but there is
a semblance of it somewhere
perhaps, in the home-cooked meals
or the late night drives
or that hot cup of chai.

there is no routine
but my days are nonchalant
nothing out of the ordinary
like a comfort TV show
watched more than once
repeating itself, over and over.
- it's stuck like a broken record.

creations

the universe comes together
in a cosmic creation of destiny
and meticulously places
everything around you.

it is not mere coincidence
that you have met the people,
visited and belonged to places,
shared the best and worst experiences.

it is all a part of our existence
that the universe deemed necessary
much like the moon and the sun
and the stars in the night sky.
- we are deliberate creations.

home(sickness)

there is a home i am sick for
but it is no tangible place
where i can simply walk in.

it is a guarded place
with walls that hold some
of the darkest corners.

there is a place i miss terribly
that is nowhere near me
and one i cannot simply walk into.

it is far, far away
and i am homesick for it
and i will be, until it returns.
- home does not need to be a place.

journeys

somebody once told me,
"you are going to
touch the moon".

how beautiful is it
to tell someone that
they are meant to go out
into the universe.

how beautiful is it
to claim somebody's existence
as one that belongs with
those like the stellar.

they told me,
"and you will go to mars,
to saturn, to neptune".
- celestial bodies belong together.

lives lived

she is beyond worlds
but also within them
wearing multiple faces,
living experiences,
honing skills of various existences.

she is beyond worlds
bearing the marks and scars
of those lives she has
lived and not lived
learned and unlearned.

she is beyond worlds
and her soul is old and wise,
for she is a writer
who has lived lives
of any and all kinds.
- she is a multiverse.

an artist's struggles

when i turn up blank
i decide that it is time
to fill myself with all things
meaningful and creative and expressive.

i yearn to soak in the world
of creativity, of inspiration
and gather the strength
of other artists who struggle like me.

- after all, art is birthed from experience.

turbulence

there may be a reason
for the constant changes
and redirections happening
in your life right now.

the world rumbles around you
turbulence occurs when there is
something in the way,
and the only way out is through it.
- it does not last forever.

acceptance

i will create a home
beyond the four walls
and the doors and windows
where we accept and celebrate
our individuality
rather than a house
that is just four walls
and doors and windows
in which we simply exist.
- i choose to accept identity over existence.

waiting for sunrise

the moon is a lovely thing
a queen among its many
glimmering, scattered subjects
across a dark horizon.

but the lack of colour
and the iridescence
reminds me much of
the way i no longer want to feel.

i want the sun-kissed sky
to greet my eyes
and feel the pinks and reds
flooding within me.

do not mistake me
i adore the lovely, white moon
but now i miss the rainbow
of colours i am made of.
- now i wait for sunrises.

a loud existence

be loud.
when you commit to yourself,
to your goals and dreams,
do it in a way that people think
a storm is coming.

be loud.
when you have a meltdown
but you pick yourself up
and dry your tears,
the thundercloud parts for a rainbow.

be loud.
when you attract positivity
and get what you desire,
you celebrate in a way that
people think the stars are quaking.
- announce your existence.

rootless

why remain rooted,
shackled to the ground
when you can reach
for the sky.

where there exists
no boundaries,
only stars to witness
your journey.

why remain limited
when there are
countless chances
to remain limitless.

where you can
find your dreams
across that ocean
of possibilities.
- chase the skies.

burn like a star

there is a fire within you
burning endlessly
consuming everything in its way.

let the embers fly free
and light fire elsewhere
breathing its light into every crevice.

unleash your passion
and watch the world burn
at your feet.
- you are a star like the sun.

www.ingramcontent.com/pod-product-compliance
Lightning Source LLC
Chambersburg PA
CBHW062111140826
49812CB00058B/1299